Life in Ancie EGYPT

by Angela McDonald

Ruby Tuesday Books

Map of the Ancient Egyptian World

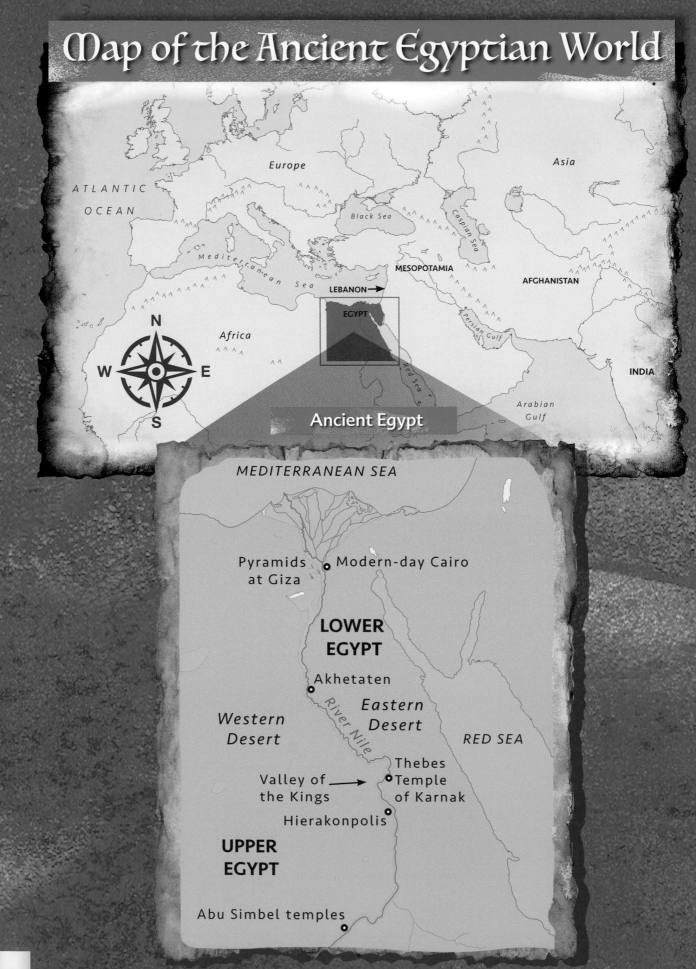

Europe

Asia

ATLANTIC OCEAN

Black Sea

Caspian Sea

MESOPOTAMIA

AFGHANISTAN

Mediterranean Sea

LEBANON →

EGYPT

Persian Gulf

Africa

Red Sea

INDIA

Arabian Gulf

N
W E
S

Ancient Egypt

MEDITERRANEAN SEA

Pyramids at Giza

Modern-day Cairo

LOWER EGYPT

Akhetaten

Eastern Desert

Western Desert

River Nile

RED SEA

Valley of the Kings →

Thebes Temple of Karnak

Hierakonpolis

UPPER EGYPT

Abu Simbel temples

Contents

Egypt's Natural Resources

Ancient Egypt was a land of plenty. Lush crops grew on its riverbanks. Gold was plentiful in its deserts. And its rocky hillsides provided stone for building.

Life-Giving Waters

Egypt's greatest treasure was the River Nile. In Egypt it hardly ever rains. Without the river's life-giving waters the country would have been nothing but dry desert.

The ancient Egyptians depended on the Nile for drinking water, growing crops and transport.

A rock containing gold

Who Were the Ancient Egyptians?

The ancient Egyptians were a powerful and wealthy civilisation that lived in Africa more than 4000 years ago. They lived along the banks of the River Nile in cities and villages and on farms. Their kings built magnificent temples, pyramids and other monuments.

The Inundation

Every year, heavy rains fell to the south of Egypt. As the Nile flowed north, it brought a torrent of southern rainwater to Egypt. The swollen river overflowed its banks, soaking Egypt's dry, sandy land with rich **minerals** that fertilised the soil. This annual flood was called the **inundation**. When the floodwaters dropped, crops could be planted in the fields along the river's banks.

Hard Stones, Precious Stones

Lots of ancient Egyptian monuments are made of sandstone and limestone that was easily cut from the desert hills. For hard rock like granite and diorite, kings sent their craftsmen to **quarries** throughout Egypt to fetch these beautiful, rarer stones.

A statue of King Khafre made of diorite

Importing Missing Treasures

The ancient Egyptians traded with other countries to get the things they needed and desired.

Egyptian trees were thin and straggly, so cedar wood from Lebanon was prized for shipbuilding.

Lapis lazuli

Egyptian artists and jewellery-makers loved to use silver from Mesopotamia and a blue rock called lapis lazuli from Afghanistan.

Exotic animals like giraffes and leopards were brought from southern Africa for their skins.

A tomb painting showing a giraffe

The Guardians

Ancient Egypt's many gods and goddesses looked after the worlds of the living and the dead.

The Creator Gods

Each Egyptian city told its own story about how the world began. In Memphis, the craftsman god Ptah created all things by imagining them and giving them names. In Aswan, the ram-god Khnum created humans on his potter's wheel.

Air, Moisture, Sky and Earth

In the city of Heliopolis, people believed the world began with the god Shu (air) and the goddess Tefnut (moisture). Shu and Tefnut had two children, Nut (sky) and Geb (Earth).

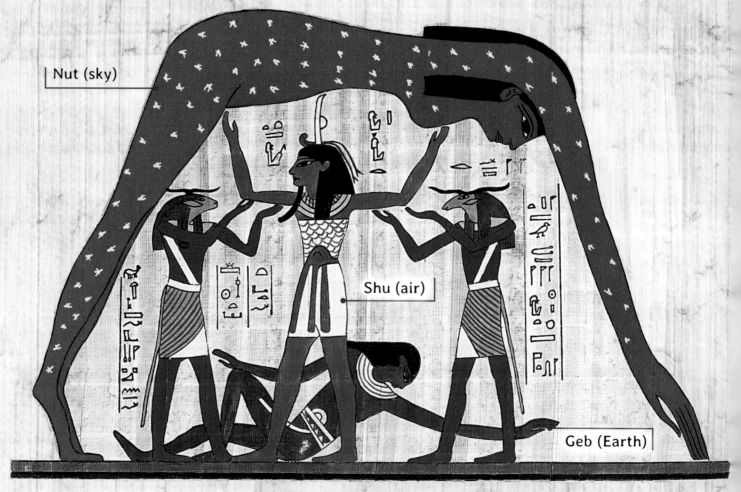

Nut (sky)

Shu (air)

Geb (Earth)

Shu loved his daughter Nut so much that he raised her high up above himself. Nut stretched herself over her family and became the starry sky, watching over them and keeping them safe forever.

Gods of the Afterlife

The god Osiris was killed by his brother Seth, who cut him into 14 pieces. Anubis, the jackal god, protected Osiris's body by drying it out. He bound the pieces back together with bandages and made the first **mummy**. Then Osiris was brought back to life by the magical powers of his sisters Isis and Nephthys.

Anubis

Osiris

Osiris became the ruler of the **afterlife**. When ancient Egyptians died, they hoped to live in his kingdom with their bodies **preserved** and their **souls** alive again.

Guard Gods

Women and children wore **amulets** believed to offer the protection of Bes and Tawaret. These gods scared harmful things away from people and houses. The goddess Hathor had many temples outside Egypt. She looked after lonely travellers if they felt homesick.

Bes amulet

Tawaret amulet

Balance and Opposites

The Egyptians believed in opposite forces balancing each other, even among the gods.

The inundation god Hapi brought life.

The crocodile god Sobek stole life away.

Bread, Beer and Fabulous Feasts

Fruit trees, cereal crops and many other plants flourished in Egypt, giving the ancient Egyptians both everyday foods and special treats.

The Cycle of Life

The Egyptian year had three seasons, each divided into four months. In *Akhet* (inundation), the Nile overflowed and fertilised its banks. In *Peret* (growing), the waters retreated and crops were planted to grow in the fertilised soil. By the end of *Shemu* (harvest) crops were harvested before the cycle began again.

Fishermen

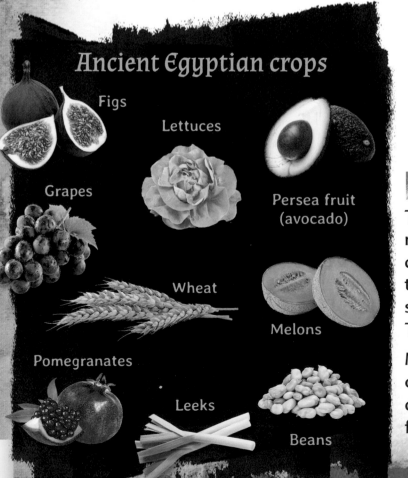

Ancient Egyptian crops

Figs

Lettuces

Grapes

Persea fruit (avocado)

Wheat

Melons

Pomegranates

Leeks

Beans

The Nile was teeming with fish. People also hunted turtles and water birds such as ducks in the river.

Food for the Rich and the Poor

The rich feasted on exotic roasted meats such as pigeon, quail — and sometimes even hyena! They tucked into oily persea fruits, sticky sycamore figs and tasty cakes. They also drank luxurious wines.

Most ordinary Egyptians survived on bread made from emmer wheat and a thick, soupy beer made from barley.

Mash

Beer

Barley

Beer-makers strain a mash of water and barley through cloth to make beer.

Uncovering Secret Recipes

In cities such as Hierakonpolis and Tell el Farka **archaeologists** have found the remains of huge breweries. Some were able to produce nearly 400 litres of beer a day! By studying the gunky remains inside the cooking vats, we can tell several different recipes were used. Most included wheat and barley and some were sweetened with nabq fruit.

A Final Feast

Thanks to the work of archaeologists we now know what Egyptian princesses ate 5000 years ago. Princess Shepsesipet was about 60 years old when she died. Inside her tomb, archaeologists found her family's footprints around her coffin. They also found and analysed remains of the feast that the princess's family had placed in the tomb for her to enjoy in the afterlife.

Bread

Porridge

Nabq fruit

Beef ribs

Quail

Kidneys

Stewed figs

Honey cakes

Roasted pigeon

Fish

Beef legs

The King

**To the Egyptian people their king was like a god.
And only he could speak directly to the gods.**

Duties and Dangers

Ancient Egyptian kings, or **pharaohs**, faced danger every day. They fought wars in faraway lands to protect Egypt from her enemies. And at home there was the danger of **ambitious** men who wanted power.

In one famous story, the ghost of King Amenemhat I warns his son not to trust anyone. That's because Amenemhat had been murdered by his own bodyguards!

The English word "pharaoh" comes from *per aah*, which means "palace" in Egyptian.

Giant statues of Pharaoh Ramses II at the temple of Abu Simbel

Kingdoms and Dynasties

Ancient Egyptian history is divided into a timeline of three Kingdoms — Old, Middle and New. The timeline is then divided again into families of kings called dynasties. A pharaoh's eldest son expected to become the next king. And every king wanted to be richer, stronger and more impressive than the one before.

Kingdoms of Ancient Egypt
The times between the Kingdoms are known as Intermediate Periods.

Old Kingdom 2575 - 2150 BC	Middle Kingdom 2055 - 1650 BC	New Kingdom 1550 - 1069 BC

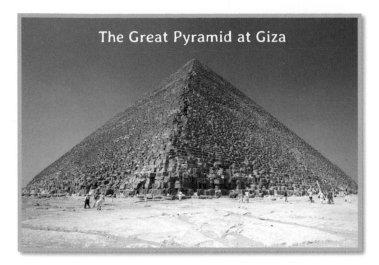
The Great Pyramid at Giza

In the Old Kingdom, pharaohs built enormous pyramids to be their tombs. Khufu's pyramid at Giza is the largest. It contains 2.3 million limestone blocks and is the height of a 40-storey building.

The New Kingdom was the age of enormous temples, such as Karnak in Thebes. This temple was the home of the god Amun. New Kingdom kings kept adding more sections to the temple until it was as big as a city!

What's in a Name?

Kings had five royal names. A king's two most important names – his birth name and his throne name – were written in **hieroglyphs** inside an oval called a *cartouche*. A king was given his throne name when he came to power.

Tutankhamun's birth name   Tutankhamun's throne name

A reconstruction of the temple at Karnak

A Female King

In the 18th dynasty (around 1450 BC), two unusual kings ruled Egypt together – a young boy Thutmosis III and his stepmother Hatshepsut. Thutmosis was too young to rule alone, so Hatshepsut was his protector. Eventually, however, she made herself king! During her reign, Hatshepsut built many splendid temples. But after she died and Thutmosis came to power, her buildings and statues were mysteriously destroyed. Did Thutmosis take revenge on his stepmother for stealing his throne?

Hatshepsut's statues show her as a male king – she even has a beard!

Jobs in Ancient Egypt

In ancient Egypt, men went out to work, while most women took care of their house and family.

In Charge of Breakfast and Cakes

We learn about the jobs some people did by the titles they used. Important officials often had dozens of different titles. Some tell us exactly what a job involved — for example, "Overseer of the King's Breakfast", "Maker of Stone Vases" or "Chief of the Thousands and Thousands of Cakes".

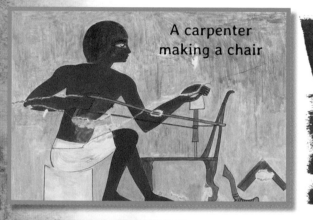

A carpenter making a chair

Running the Country

One of the most important jobs was vizier – the king's prime minister. The vizier collected taxes, settled law cases and managed the king's building projects. It wasn't only men who did this important job. A small number of women did, too.

Serving the King

Some ancient Egyptians became soldiers, priests, doctors, **architects** or **scribes**. But most people were farmers.

Every Egyptian was the king's servant and he could command them to do anything he liked. When they weren't needed in the fields, farmers worked for their king as labourers building pyramids and temples.

Highly skilled artists created the tomb paintings that tell us so much about ancient Egyptian life.

A farmer herds cattle

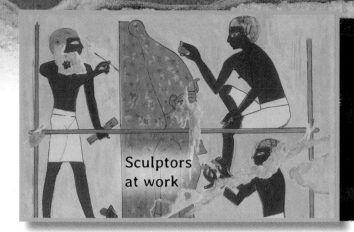
Sculptors at work

Master Makers

The king had hundreds of craftsmen working for him. Stonemasons cut and shaped rock for building. Sculptors carved statues and carpenters built ships and furniture. Jewellers created beautiful objects from gold and precious stones.

Life for Slaves

Slaves in ancient Egypt were usually captives from other countries who became the property of temples, high-powered officials and the king. For some slaves daily life meant hard work and painful beatings. But the slaves of some wealthy families probably lived in more comfort than a poor farmer and became part of the family they served.

Ancient Egyptian Comedy

A song called "The Satire of the Trades" makes fun of every job. Reed-cutters get eaten by mosquitoes, gardeners get hunched shoulders, farmers are stinky and fishermen will probably end up inside a crocodile!

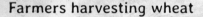
Farmers harvesting wheat

A child helps with the work.

Block of stone for a pyramid

Labourers hauled blocks of stone.

A Child's World

Ancient Egyptian children had to grow up quickly!

Off to Work

As soon as they were old enough, boys worked alongside adults learning the same jobs as their fathers. Mothers trained their daughters to weave cloth and cook. Both boys and girls worked in the fields, planting and harvesting crops.

Childhood Deaths

Nearly half of all children died before they were five years old.
They caught dangerous infections or were bitten by snakes and scorpions.
Curiously archaeologists rarely find children in ancient Egyptian cemeteries.
Instead, young children were often buried under the floor of their family's house.
Were they too young to be left in a cemetery on their own?
Or could their families just not bear to part with them?

Becoming a Scribe

In ancient Egypt highly trained scribes did most of the reading and writing. They kept records for kings, government officials, the army and priests. They also wrote down spells that people could buy to put into coffins or carry for protection. The sons of scribes went to special schools to learn hieroglyphs and become scribes like their fathers.

Boys copied out texts written by their teacher. They practised writing on pieces of stone or broken pottery.

Once they were skilled, trainee scribes wrote on **papyrus** paper with reeds dipped in ink.

Ancient Toys

Toys such as marbles and balls have been found in children's graves. So have little clay animals and human figures. But were these doll-like objects actually toys? Archaeologists think they may have been placed in the grave for magical or religious reasons.

An ancient Egyptian ball made of linen and string

Ancient Egyptian paintings show us most of what we know about children. They are shown as small, usually naked figures with a long plaited pigtail on the side of their heads. While some art shows children playing, it's far more common to see them at work.

The plait was called the sidelock of youth.

Writing with Hieroglyphs

The ancient Egyptians believed the god Thoth invented hieroglyphs. They called writing "god's words".

Mysterious Pictures

For hundreds of years, **scholars** and **Egyptologists** tried to figure out how hieroglyphs worked. At first, some people tried to read them as pictures or ideas. For example, they thought the owl hieroglyph stood for "death", perhaps because owls hunt and kill.

Owl hieroglyph

The god Thoth

Solving a Puzzle

In the 1820s, a French scholar named Jean-François Champollion was one of the first people to decode hieroglyphs with the help of a slab of stone with carved texts called the Rosetta Stone. He discovered that many of the symbols on the stone represented sounds and not just ideas. For example, the owl hieroglyph actually stands for "m".

Rosetta Stone

Hieroglyphs

Demotic

Ancient Greek

The Rosetta Stone

The Rosetta Stone was discovered in Egypt in 1799. Carved onto the stone is the same piece of text in three different types of writing – ancient Greek, **Demotic** and hieroglyphs. Jean-François Champollion knew how to read ancient Greek. Therefore, by comparing the Greek version of the text to the hieroglyphic version, he was able to decipher some of the symbols – just like cracking a code!

How to Read Hieroglyphs

There are three types of hieroglyphs:
- **Phonograms (sound signs)**
- **Determinatives (meaning signs)**
- **Logograms (sound and meaning signs)**

Hieroglyphic words can be written left to right, right to left or top to bottom.

Phonograms

Phonograms represent a sound and are a little like the letters in our alphabet. For example, the ancient Egyptian word for "crocodile" was *meseh*. It's written using the phonograms for m, s and h (we add in the letter "e" so it's possible for us to pronounce the word).

m e s e h (determinative)

To help show the word's meaning a sign of a crocodile (the determinative) is added.

s
r

These hieroglyphs write the word *ser*, which means "to tell the future". Its determinative is a giraffe – because giraffes are tall enough to see things coming before anyone else can!

Logograms

Logograms are sound and meaning signs. This logogram means "star" and its sound is *seba*.

The meanings of these logograms are:

Water   Leg   Cry   Wind   House

k
n
d

These hieroglyphs write the word *kened*, which means "to be angry". It has a baboon determinative because baboons are usually fierce, angry creatures.

Letters to the Dead

A letter to the dead

Sometimes hieroglyphic texts are found on unusual materials, like a magical spell written on a human skull, or letters found in tombs that were written to ghosts on pottery bowls. It was believed that the dead could be powerful. Therefore a person who was suffering a misfortune, such as ill health, would write to a dead relative and ask for help from beyond the grave.

Protecting Yourself

When illness or injury struck, the ancient Egyptians believed that dark forces were plotting against them. To fight the darkness, they turned to medicine, magic or a combination of both.

Honey, a Pig's Tooth and Donkey Dung

Ancient Egyptian recipes for medicine tell us how doctors treated their patients. For indigestion, the cure was eating a pig's tooth, crushed and baked into a cake!

Some ingredients we actually still use today. For example, honey was used to treat coughs. Other ingredients we'd never dream of using, like worm blood cooked with donkey dung and mole to soothe a splinter.

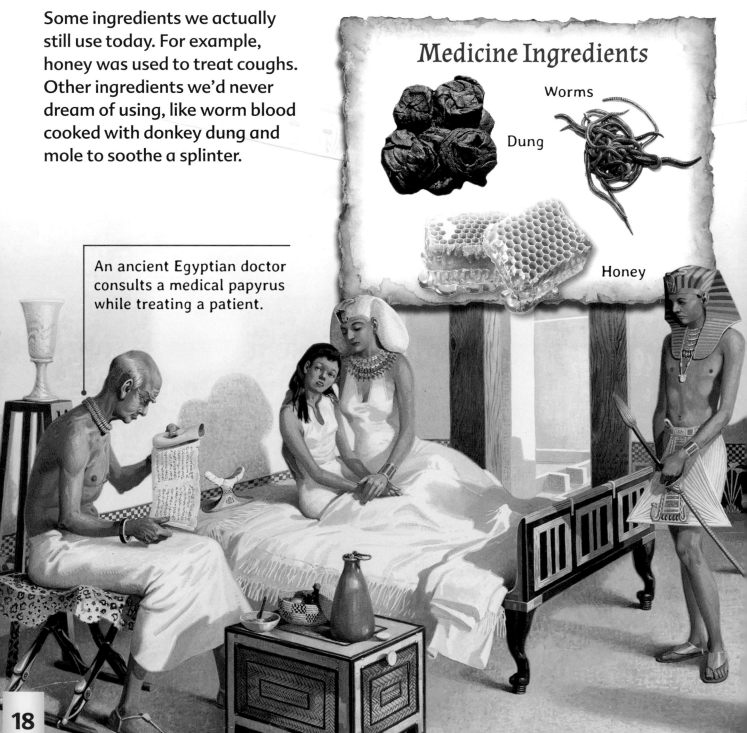

Medicine Ingredients

Worms

Dung

Honey

An ancient Egyptian doctor consults a medical papyrus while treating a patient.

The Gods Are Angry!

Blindness was very common in ancient Egypt. It was known as "seeing darkness by day". People believed that angry gods could make them go blind. They offered the gods gifts of food and jewellery to let them see again.

One man thought he'd gone blind and been cursed because he'd eaten tripe (the stomach of a cow) when he'd promised not to. He wrote a letter on papyrus to his mother promising her and the gods that he'd never do it again.

Mummified foot

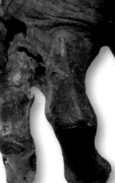

A doctor or craftsman made this person a prosthetic, or false, wooden toe.

The Eye of Horus

One of the most powerful protective amulets was called the *wedjat*. It could protect the person who wore it from anything. The *wedjat* was supposed to be the eye of the god Horus. Seth and Horus fought over who would be king and Seth cut out Horus's eye. Horus's mother, Isis, healed the eye with gazelle's milk and magic.

This ancient Egyptian papyrus is the world's oldest surviving surgical record. ▼

The notes include how to stitch wounds and how to stop bleeding using raw meat.

The Magic of Dreams

There's a papyrus that tells us how the ancient Egyptians interpreted their dreams. For example, if you dreamed about looking out of a window, your prayers would be answered. But if you dreamed about looking into a deep well, it meant going to prison!

Life After Death

After death, people in ancient Egypt hoped for an afterlife in the kingdom of Osiris.

The *ba* had a human face and the body of a bird.

The *Ka* and *Ba*

The ancient Egyptians believed that every person was born with a *ka*, a ghostly copy of themselves that came alive after death. Like a living person, the *ka* needed to eat, drink and be kept comfortable. A person also had a *ba*, which gave the dead the power to move in the afterlife.

In order for a person to live on in the afterlife, their *ka* and *ba* had to stay with their body.

To make a mummy, a dead body was dried by covering it with natron salt. Then the dry, shrivelled body was wrapped in linen bandages.

To preserve a dead body and keep it safe, it was mummified and laid in a tomb. Then food and drink were placed in the tomb for the *ka*. However, only the wealthy could afford a tomb. Ordinary Egyptians were simply laid in graves dug in the ground.

The Final Judgement

The dead had to face Osiris in the Hall of Justice. Here, a person's heart was weighed against the feather of justice. During life, a person's heart soaked up all of their good and bad deeds. A good heart would weigh lighter than the feather, allowing its owner to enter Osiris's kingdom. A bad heart was heavier and would be gobbled up by the Devourer monster. Its owner would disappear and never reach the afterlife!

The weighing of the heart ceremony

Anubis

Heart

Feather of justice

Forever Perfect

Mummification aimed to keep bodies perfect – and fix imperfect ones. Mummies have been found with dyed hair and even false legs to replace limbs that were missing in life. A beautiful mask was added to the bandaged body to make sure the mummy's face looked perfect.

The Devourer monster was part crocodile, part lion and part hippo.

A wig of human hair

A mummy mask

Tomb Secrets

Most of what we know about ancient Egypt comes from tombs.

Ready for the Afterlife

The Egyptians believed they could take their possessions with them into the afterlife. Clothes, shoes, furniture — all the things a person used in life were placed in their tomb. Wealthy Egyptians were also buried with jewellery, gold and other treasures.

Hidden Treasures

The architect Kha was buried with nearly 200 objects, ranging from perfumes and sandals to the measuring tools he used in his job.

Model of a butcher's workshop

A Miniature World

In the tomb of a man named Meketre, archaeologists discovered a secret chamber. It was filled with tiny, brightly painted, realistic wooden models that included a cattle barn, a granary and servants busily working in a butcher's workshop. Like a miniature world, the models were placed in the tomb to give Meketre food and servants in the afterlife.

A model of Meketre's peaceful garden.

Wrapped in Secrets

Long before mummification was invented, the dead in Egypt were buried in the sand, wrapped in reeds or animal furs. The body of one older woman from Hierakonpolis was wrapped in tree bark, possibly from a frankincense tree that grew far from Egypt. The woman had died from a hard blow to the left side of her head and her hair had been carefully combed over the wound.

Bark wrappings

▲ By examining the woman's skeleton and grave we can reconstruct her burial from more than 5000 years ago.

Reading Between the Layers

Some mummy masks were made of **cartonnage**, layers of linen or papyrus covered with plaster. Sometimes mask makers used recycled papyrus that had been written on. In the past huge numbers of masks were destroyed so Egyptologists could read these texts. Now scientists are using deep-imaging to see them. By shining different types of light on a mask, they can see through the plaster and paint to the writing inked on the ancient papyri.

Cartonnage mummy mask

The Bad Guys

In ancient Egypt there were wicked people, evil demons and even bad guy gods.

A gold falcon from the tomb of Pharaoh Tutankhamun

Tomb Robbers

Some of the worst criminals were tomb robbers. These unscrupulous thieves broke into the tombs of kings, queens and wealthy Egyptians. They stole jewellery, gold and silver objects, furniture, clothes and even perfume and make-up.

The Worst Crime Possible

Sometimes, tomb robbers **desecrated** a mummy by stealing amulets from between the bandages, pulling rings from its fingers and tearing the beautiful mask from its face.

To the ancient Egyptians, robbing the tomb of a king and disturbing his mummy was the worst crime possible. The punishment for this evil deed was execution!

A damaged statue of Akhenaten

A Bad Guy King

No ancient Egyptian king was more hated than Akhenaten. He stopped his people from worshipping their **traditional** gods and made them worship a single Sun god called the Aten. He closed down all their temples and forced them to move to his new city named Akhetaten. But the unpopular pharaoh paid the price. When he died, the people destroyed Akhenaten's temples, smashed up his statues, hacked his name from wall carvings and abandoned his city!

The Two Sides of Seth

The god Seth was a bad-tempered, jealous troublemaker and murderer. However, this bad guy god did have a good side.

During the day, the Sun god Ra travelled through the sky. By night he sailed through the blackness of the underworld accompanied by Seth and other gods. Each night, just before dawn, a giant demon snake named Apophis attacked Ra to stop him rising into the sky. But every night Seth protected Ra by killing Apophis.

When dawn came, the blood of evil Apophis painted the morning sky red.

The demon Apophis

The god Seth

Tutankhamun's Tomb

In 1922, British archaeologist Howard Carter made a spectacular discovery in the Valley of the Kings — Pharaoh Tutankhamun's treasure-filled tomb.

The Valley of the Kings

By the New Kingdom (1550 BC), ancient Egyptian kings had stopped building pyramids. They were too easy to rob! Instead, their tomb builders tunnelled into the rocky hills at Thebes, creating underground spiderwebs of corridors and rooms where the kings could rest undisturbed.

This huge cemetery became known as the Valley of the Kings. A special police force called the Medjay guarded the tombs against robbers, but most tombs were eventually plundered.

Tutankhamun's Treasures

It took Carter nearly 10 years to empty Tutankhamun's tomb. Inside the tomb's four rooms were more than 5000 objects. And yet, detailed lists inside the jewellery boxes told Carter there had once been even more treasure that was now missing.

Inside the tomb Carter found jugs of wine, baskets of fruit, 130 walking sticks, model boats, sandals and eyeliner. He discovered linen underwear, a leopard skin cloak and gloves Tutankhamun had worn as a child.

A reconstruction of the first room that Carter entered in the tomb.

Chariot

Animal-shaped bed

Throne

Egg-shaped wooden boxes containing meat such as ribs, goose and an ox's tongue.

Signs of a Robbery?

When Carter found Tutankhamun's tomb it was hidden underground and had been sealed up for more than 3000 years. But Carter discovered plenty of signs that showed him the ancient tomb was a crime scene....

Tutankhamun's mummy was inside this gold coffin.

A Child King

Tutankhamun was born in around 1341 BC. It's believed he was the son of the unpopular king, Akhenaten. When Tutankhamun was still a child he became pharaoh. A few years later, when he was just 18 or 19 years old, he died.

C.S.I. King Tut's Tomb

- Items were missing from Tut's tomb, so Carter knew it had been robbed.
- But when Carter found the underground passageway that led to Tut's tomb, it was filled with rubble that Carter had to remove to get inside.
- The doors at each end of the passageway were still sealed but showed signs of earlier damage and repair.
- Look at the clues in the diagram. Can you be an archaeology detective like Carter and figure out what took place in Tut's tomb?

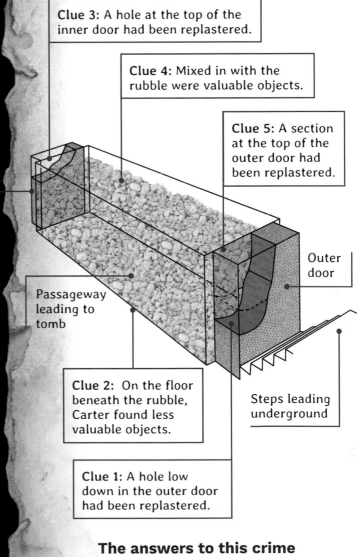

Clue 3: A hole at the top of the inner door had been replastered.

Clue 4: Mixed in with the rubble were valuable objects.

Clue 5: A section at the top of the outer door had been replastered.

Inner door leading to tomb

Outer door

Passageway leading to tomb

Clue 2: On the floor beneath the rubble, Carter found less valuable objects.

Steps leading underground

Clue 1: A hole low down in the outer door had been replastered.

The answers to this crime scene mystery are on page 32.

Archaeology and Science

Clever scientific techniques and the work of archaeologists are bringing more of ancient Egyptian life to light.

Space Archaeologist

For decades, archaeologists have taken photographs from the air to see ancient sites more clearly. But in the last 20 years, it's been possible to use satellite images taken from space. Archaeologist Sarah Parcak has used this technology to locate thousands of lost settlements and tombs in Egypt.

Sarah Parcak

A satellite orbiting Earth

Satellite images show differences and patterns in soil and rock that aren't visible at ground level.

A Lost City

One of Sarah's most exciting discoveries is Itj-tawy, the long-lost capital of Egypt during the Middle Kingdom. The satellite images showed Sarah the remains of ancient mudbrick buildings, hidden 5 metres underground.

Underground Secrets Revealed

Soil samples taken at the site have confirmed Sarah's discovery. Deep below the surface, archaeologists found traces of pottery and precious stones such as amethyst that were popular with jewellers in the Middle Kingdom.

Ancient Egyptian potters

Saved by Fire

Five thousand years ago, a fire destroyed a potter's house in the city of Hierakonpolis. Having his pottery kiln (oven) so close to the house was a disaster for the potter, but lucky for archaeologist Michael Hoffman. The house's mudbrick walls would have crumbled over time, but the fire baked them hard, leaving behind a map-like outline of the house and its outbuildings.

By analysing the charcoal and ash found at the site, Hoffman could tell the house had reed mat walls and wooden posts holding up the roof. He even found bones in the debris that suggest the potter kept donkeys, perhaps for deliveries.

Lost Underwater Worlds

A team led by archaeologist Franck Goddio has been rediscovering lost Egyptian cities such as Canopus and Heracleion that were buried deep under the ocean by a series of earthquakes. Stretches of coastline are surveyed for possible objects using **sonar** equipment. Then the team of archaeologists dive! The treasures rescued by Franck and his team range from colossal statues to tiny gold coins.

Franck Goddio

Once objects are out of the sea, the archaeologists race against time to piece together fragments of pottery, dry out waterlogged wood and remove salt which can eat away at metal and cause stone statues to crack.

This 5-metre-tall granite statue of a pharaoh was found under the ocean in five pieces.

Glossary

afterlife
The place where a person's spirit or soul lives on after death.

ambitious
Having a strong wish to be successful, powerful or rich.

amulet
A good luck charm carried or worn and believed to protect a person from harm.

archaeologist
A scientist who studies the past by examining the physical remains left behind, for example buildings, coins, weapons or skeletons.

architect
A person who designs and manages the construction of buildings and other structures.

cartonnage
A material made of layers of linen or papyrus and wet plaster. When the mixture dries, it goes hard like papier-mâché.

civilisation
A large group of people from a particular area that share the same history, culture and way of life.

Demotic
A form of everyday writing used in ancient Egypt.

desecrate
Violently damage or treat with disrespect, especially in connection with something highly valued or considered sacred.

Egyptologist
A person who studies the ancient Egyptians.

hieroglyphs
The writing of ancient Egypt. A hieroglyph is a sign that has a meaning or stands for a sound.

inundation
The annual flooding of the River Nile. The flood waters fertilised the soil and made the growing of crops possible.

mineral
A solid material that is formed by natural processes and is found in soil or water. For example, iron and calcium are both minerals needed by plants.

monument
A statue, building or other structure that is erected to commemorate a person or event.

mummy
The dead (and usually ancient) body of a person or animal where bones and soft tissues, such as skin, have been preserved.

papyrus
Tall, reed-like plants with stems that can be crushed to make paper.

pharaoh
A king in ancient Egypt.

preserve
To protect something and stop it from being damaged or destroyed.

quarry
A large deep hole from which rock, such as granite, is dug out.

scholar
A person who studies and is highly educated.

scribe
A person (usually a man) who could read and write.

sonar
A system for detecting objects underwater. Sonar equipment emits sound pulses that bounce off objects underwater and can then be detected and measured.

soul
The spirit, or non-physical, part of a human or animal that is believed to live on after death.

traditional
Something that has been a custom, belief or practice for a long time and has been passed on from one generation to the next.

This famous limestone bust depicts Queen Nefertiti. She was the chief wife of Pharaoh Akhenaten and stepmother to Tutankhamun. Nefertiti's tomb and mummy have not yet been found. ▼

Index

ANSWERS: C.S.I. King Tut's Tomb (page 27)

Howard Carter realised that the tomb had been robbed twice!

Clue 1: At the time of the first robbery, the passageway was empty. The thieves had been able to climb in by making the lower hole in the outer door.

Clue 3: The thieves entered the tomb by making a hole in the top of the inner door.

Clue 2: As the thieves escaped, they discarded less valuable objects (that were not worth stealing) onto the floor of the passageway.

After the first robbery, the tomb guards quickly filled the passageway with rubble and replastered and sealed the doors.

Clue 5: A second gang of robbers had to make a hole in the top of the outer door so they could crawl in over the rubble. They made a hole in the inner door at the same spot as the first gang.

Clue 4: As the second gang crawled back over the rubble to escape, they accidentally dropped valuable objects that slipped between the chunks of rubble.